The Emotion Code

Unlocking the Power of Emotional Intelligence

By **Anil Solanki**

Copyright © 2024 Anil Solanki

All rights reserved. No part of this book may be reproduced, distributed, or transmitted in any form or by any means, including photocopying, recording, or other electronic or mechanical methods, without the prior written permission of the author, except in the case of brief quotations embodied in critical reviews and certain other non-commercial uses permitted by copyright law.

ISBN: 9798343238938

Self-Published on Amazon KDP

Disclaimer:
This book is intended for informational and educational purposes only. It is not a substitute for professional advice or therapy. The author disclaims any liability for any damages or negative consequences from any action taken based on this book. Always consult a professional before making decisions that may affect your health, well-being, or personal circumstances.

Dedication
To all those who seek a deeper understanding of themselves and others. May this journey help you unlock the full potential of your emotional intelligence.

Introduction: The Power of Emotional Intelligence

We live in an age where knowledge is readily available, where technology and automation drive progress, and where IQ is often seen as the primary predictor of success. But in our ever-evolving world, there is an element that is often overlooked, yet plays a vital role in our personal and professional lives—emotional intelligence (EQ).

Emotional intelligence is the ability to recognize, understand, manage, and harness emotions in ourselves and others. It is what allows us to navigate relationships, handle stress, and make decisions with empathy and clarity. While IQ might help us solve problems, EQ helps us connect with others, lead with compassion, and stay resilient in the face of challenges.

I've always believed that emotional intelligence is one of the most valuable skills anyone can develop, not just for success in work but for living a fulfilling, meaningful life. Unlike IQ, which is relatively fixed, EQ can be learned and improved at any stage of life. It helps us become more self-aware, empathize with others, regulate our emotions, and make thoughtful decisions, even in the most challenging situations.

In this book, we will dive deep into the components of emotional intelligence and how they impact every aspect of our lives. From improving personal relationships to becoming a more effective leader at work, EQ is the foundation upon which true growth and success are built.

You'll learn:
- **What emotional intelligence is and why it matters.**
- **How EQ can transform personal and professional relationships.**
- **Practical strategies for developing self-awareness, emotional control, and empathy.**
- **How emotional intelligence enhances leadership and decision-making.**
- **Techniques to continuously cultivate and strengthen your EQ.**

As you progress through the chapters, you'll find actionable insights and exercises to help you implement emotional intelligence in your daily life. Whether you're striving to improve your communication with loved ones, advance in your career, or simply become more emotionally balanced, this book will serve as your guide.

Emotional intelligence is not a destination but a journey—one that requires self-reflection, practice, and a genuine desire to grow. But as you'll discover, it is a journey well worth taking.

So, let's begin. Let's unlock the power of emotional intelligence and open the door to deeper connections, greater success, and a more fulfilling life.

Welcome to the journey.

Table of Contents

By **Anil Solanki** 1

Introduction: The Power of Emotional Intelligence 3

Chapter 1: What is Emotional Intelligence (EQ)? 10

    What is EQ? 10

    Components of EQ 11

        1. Self-Awareness 11

        2. Self-Regulation 12

        3. Motivation 13

        4. Empathy 13

        5. Social Skills 14

    The Importance of EQ 15

        EQ in Relationships 16

        EQ in Leadership 16

        EQ and Life Satisfaction 17

Chapter 2: The Role of Emotional Intelligence in Personal and Professional Relationships 19

    EQ in Personal Relationships 19

        Managing Conflicts with EQ 20

        Improving Communication 21

        Building Stronger, Empathetic Relationships 21

    EQ in the Workplace 22

        Leadership and EQ 22

        Teamwork and Collaboration 23

        Decision-Making and Job Performance 24

Chapter 3: Developing Self-Awareness 25

Understanding Your Emotions 25
   Practical Exercise: Journaling for Emotional Awareness 26
   Using Mindfulness to Increase Self-Awareness 27
Recognizing Emotional Triggers 28
   Identifying Your Emotional Triggers 28
   The Role of Past Experiences 29
   Managing Emotional Triggers 29
Building Emotional Insight 31
   Deepening Emotional Insight through Reflection 31
   Meditation and Mindfulness for Emotional Insight 32
   Seeking Feedback for Greater Insight 33
   Embracing Vulnerability for Emotional Growth 34

Chapter 4: Cultivating Emotional Control 35
   The Power of Pause 35
   The Pause in High-Stress Situations 36
   Pausing Before Important Decisions 37
   Managing Stress and Anxiety 38
   The Impact of Stress on Emotions 38
   Breathing Techniques for Instant Calm 39
   Healthy Outlets for Stress 40
   The Role of Routine in Managing Stress 40
   Practicing Emotional Regulation 41
   Recognizing the Importance of Regulation 42
   Techniques for Emotional Regulation 42
      Regulating Emotions in the Workplace 43

Real-Time Emotional Control 44

Why Emotional Regulation Matters 44

Chapter 5: Enhancing Empathy 46

Active Listening 46

How to Listen Actively 47

Avoiding Distractions 48

The Impact of Active Listening 48

Perspective-Taking 49

Why Perspective-Taking Matters 49

How to Practice Perspective-Taking 51

Overcoming Biases and Assumptions 52

The Benefits of Perspective-Taking 52

Cultivating Compassion 53

What is Compassion? 53

    How Compassion Enhances Relationships 54

    Practicing Compassion in Everyday Life 55

    Compassion as a Leadership Quality 56

    Compassion as a Path to Emotional Healing 56

    The Ripple Effect of Compassion 57

Chapter 6: Building Stronger Relationships through EQ 58

Improving Communication 58

    Clarity in Communication 58

    Openness in Conversations 60

Non-Defensive Responses 61

Conclusion: A New Approach to Communication 62

Navigating Conflict with EQ 62
    Staying Calm Under Pressure 63
    Listening with Empathy 64
    Focusing on Solutions, Not Blame 64
    Owning Your Part 65
    Finding Common Ground 66
Conclusion: Turning Conflict into Connection 66
Developing Social Awareness 67
Understanding Group Dynamics 67
Reading Non-Verbal Cues 68
Building Rapport and Connection 69
Navigating Social Situations with Empathy 70
Conclusion: Social Awareness as a Tool for Connection
.... 71

Chapter 7: Emotional Intelligence in Leadership 72

Leading with Empathy 72
    How to Lead with Empathy: 73
Decision-Making with Emotional Intelligence 74
    How EQ Enhances Decision-Making: 74
Building Emotionally Intelligent Teams 75
    Key Strategies for Building Emotionally Intelligent
    Teams: 76

Chapter 8: Lifelong EQ Growth 78

Continuous Self-Reflection 78
Practicing Emotional Intelligence Daily 80
    1. Start Each Day with Emotional Check-Ins 81

- 2. Pause Before Reacting 81
- 3. Practice Active Listening 81
- 4. Use Gratitude as a Tool 82
- 5. Manage Stress Proactively...................................82
- 6. Acknowledge Your Progress 82
- Final Words of Encouragement 83
- Call to Action 85
- Author's Note...87
  - Contact Information..88
    - Email: 88
    - Website: 88
    - Social Media:...89

Chapter 1: What is Emotional Intelligence (EQ)?

In my own journey of personal and professional growth, one of the most transformative realizations I've had is the power of emotional intelligence (EQ). Over time, I've learned that while intelligence quotient (IQ) may open doors, emotional intelligence determines whether you stay in the room and thrive. In today's fast-paced, interconnected world, emotional intelligence has become a cornerstone for success, not just in business, but in all aspects of life.

What is EQ?

At its core, emotional intelligence is the ability to recognize, understand, and manage our own emotions, while also being attuned to the emotions of others. It involves balancing both self-awareness and empathy to navigate through complex emotional landscapes—both within us and in our interactions with others.

In my own life, I've noticed how often people focus on intellect and logic, while underestimating the power of emotions. For example, in situations where a colleague was struggling to meet deadlines, I used to offer logical solutions—time management strategies or productivity hacks. But it wasn't until I learned to tap into emotional intelligence that I realized the root of their struggle was emotional—stress, burnout, or lack of motivation.

By recognizing and addressing those emotions, I could offer a more compassionate and effective approach.

EQ isn't just about managing feelings; it's about understanding the role emotions play in influencing thoughts, behaviors, and decisions. It's about being able to control impulsive reactions, recognize emotional triggers, and respond in a way that builds trust and collaboration.

Components of EQ

As I delved deeper into emotional intelligence, I realized that EQ is not just a single skill, but a combination of several interconnected abilities. These components work together to help us understand and manage both our emotions and the emotions of those around us. In my experience, mastering these components has not only improved my emotional well-being but also enhanced my relationships and professional success.

1. Self-Awareness

Self-awareness is the foundation of emotional intelligence. It's the ability to recognize and understand our own emotions as they occur. Early in my journey, I often found myself reacting emotionally without really understanding why. Frustration would boil over, or I'd feel anxious in certain situations, but I couldn't pinpoint the source.

When I began to develop self-awareness, I started paying attention to how I felt in specific moments and asking myself deeper questions: *What exactly am I feeling right now? Why am I feeling this way?* This practice gave me clarity, allowing me to identify triggers and patterns in my emotional responses.

For instance, I noticed that I would become defensive when receiving constructive criticism. With self-awareness, I learned to recognize this emotional reaction and gradually shift my perspective, understanding that feedback wasn't an attack but an opportunity for growth.

2. Self-Regulation

Once I gained a clearer understanding of my emotions, the next step was learning to manage them—this is where self-regulation comes into play. Self-regulation is about controlling our emotional responses in a way that's appropriate for the situation. For me, this was about taking a pause when I felt anger, frustration, or anxiety building up.

In moments when I felt overwhelmed, instead of reacting impulsively, I practiced techniques like deep breathing or stepping away for a moment of reflection. These small actions made a big difference in how I handled stress. Self-regulation also involves staying calm under pressure, managing impulsive reactions, and maintaining focus on long-term goals, even when emotions try to steer you off course.

Over time, I learned that self-regulation isn't about suppressing emotions; it's about acknowledging them and choosing how to respond. It's a skill that has been invaluable in both my personal relationships and professional life.

3. Motivation

Motivation, in the context of emotional intelligence, is the inner drive that pushes us toward our goals. It's about finding a deep sense of purpose and staying committed, even in the face of setbacks. Personally, I've found that those who excel in EQ are often highly motivated by their own values and long-term aspirations rather than external rewards.

There have been moments in my life when motivation faltered, especially when faced with challenges that seemed insurmountable. But I learned that emotional intelligence helps you stay connected to your "why"—the reason behind your goals. When you're clear on your purpose, setbacks become easier to overcome because they don't define you; they refine you.

For me, maintaining this level of motivation required a shift in mindset. Instead of being discouraged by obstacles, I began to see them as opportunities to grow. This optimistic outlook is a hallmark of high emotional intelligence and is crucial for sustaining long-term success.

4. Empathy

Empathy is, in many ways, the cornerstone of emotional intelligence. It's the ability to understand and share the feelings of others. Developing empathy has been transformative for me, both personally and professionally. It goes beyond just feeling bad for someone—it's about putting yourself in their shoes and truly understanding their perspective.

In the early stages of my EQ journey, I realized that I wasn't always the best listener. I would often jump to conclusions or offer solutions without fully understanding the other person's emotions. But as I worked on developing empathy, I became a better listener. I began to ask more questions, really tune in to what others were feeling, and offer support that was aligned with their needs.

Empathy has deepened my relationships, helping me connect with others on a more meaningful level. Whether in the workplace or at home, it has allowed me to navigate difficult conversations with grace and understanding, leading to stronger bonds and more effective communication.

5. Social Skills

Finally, social skills represent the outward expression of emotional intelligence. Once we have developed self-awareness, self-regulation, motivation, and empathy, we can effectively apply these abilities in our interactions with others. In my experience, strong social skills have been the key to building lasting relationships, resolving conflicts, and fostering collaboration.

Social skills are about more than just being friendly or charismatic; they involve clear communication, active listening, and the ability to navigate complex social situations. For example, in my professional life, I've found that effective leadership depends heavily on social skills—understanding team dynamics, resolving conflicts with tact, and motivating others to work toward a common goal.

Whether in casual conversations or high-stakes negotiations, emotional intelligence has helped me develop the social skills necessary to connect with others in a meaningful way. It's about being present, showing empathy, and communicating with authenticity.

Now that we've explored the components of emotional intelligence, let's turn our attention to why EQ is so crucial in today's world. In the next section, I'll discuss **The Importance of EQ**, where we'll dive into how emotional intelligence impacts our relationships, leadership, and overall life satisfaction.

The Importance of EQ

Over the years, I've come to realize that emotional intelligence is one of the most powerful predictors of success in both personal and professional life. While IQ can help you solve problems and think critically, it's EQ that enables you to navigate the complex emotional landscapes of relationships, work environments, and everyday interactions.

The more I developed my own emotional intelligence, the clearer it became: EQ is not just important—it's essential. In this section, I'll explain why EQ is crucial for relationships, leadership, and overall life satisfaction, based on my personal experiences and observations.

EQ in Relationships

Relationships, whether personal or professional, thrive on communication, trust, and empathy. I've found that when emotional intelligence is high, relationships become stronger, more fulfilling, and less prone to conflict. For example, in my early years, I struggled to understand the emotional cues of others. This often led to miscommunications and even disagreements that could have been avoided with better emotional awareness.

However, as I became more attuned to my own emotions and more empathetic toward others, I noticed a significant shift. I was able to listen more actively, respond more thoughtfully, and connect with people on a deeper level. Whether it's with friends, family, or colleagues, emotional intelligence helps you understand what others are feeling and what they truly need from you.

In my relationships, the ability to recognize when someone is stressed, upset, or joyful has made all the difference. I've learned how to adjust my approach depending on the situation—sometimes offering support, sometimes giving space, and sometimes just listening without judgment. It's this emotional flexibility that has allowed my relationships to flourish.

EQ in Leadership

In my professional life, I've seen how emotional intelligence sets great leaders apart from average ones. A leader with high EQ is not only able to manage their own emotions but also navigate the emotions of their team. I've witnessed leaders who were technically brilliant but lacked emotional intelligence. They struggled to connect with their teams, which led to low morale and high turnover.

On the other hand, leaders with high EQ inspire loyalty, foster collaboration, and create environments where people feel valued and understood. I remember working under a manager who had mastered emotional intelligence. He didn't just care about the tasks at hand— he cared about the people. He made time to check in with us, not just on our work but on how we were doing as individuals.

This experience taught me that emotional intelligence in leadership is about more than just managing a team. It's about creating a space where people feel emotionally safe, respected, and motivated to do their best work. When I stepped into leadership roles, I made it a priority to develop my EQ. The result? A more cohesive team, less conflict, and higher productivity.

EQ and Life Satisfaction

Perhaps the most important lesson I've learned about emotional intelligence is how it affects our overall life satisfaction. When I was younger, I thought success was all about achieving external goals—getting a promotion, hitting financial milestones, or acquiring material things. But as I developed my emotional intelligence, I realized that true fulfillment comes from within.

EQ has helped me find greater peace and contentment by enabling me to manage stress, build meaningful relationships, and stay motivated through life's challenges. By learning to regulate my emotions, I've been able to navigate difficult situations with more grace and resilience. I've found that the ability to stay calm under pressure and bounce back from setbacks is one of the greatest gifts of emotional intelligence.

In my journey, the pursuit of emotional intelligence has been deeply rewarding. It's allowed me to experience more joy, reduce anxiety, and maintain a sense of balance, even when life gets overwhelming. While IQ might help you succeed in certain technical areas, it's EQ that leads to a more satisfying, well-rounded life.

With this foundation, we've seen how emotional intelligence plays a vital role in relationships, leadership, and overall well-being. As we move forward, we'll dive deeper into how you can **develop and enhance your emotional intelligence** in the next chapter, offering practical strategies and tools that I've personally used along my own journey.

Chapter 2: The Role of Emotional Intelligence in Personal and Professional Relationships

As I've delved deeper into understanding emotional intelligence, one thing has become abundantly clear: EQ is the cornerstone of healthy, fulfilling relationships—both personal and professional. Whether it's navigating disagreements with loved ones or collaborating with colleagues at work, emotional intelligence shapes how we connect, communicate, and thrive within our relationships. In this chapter, we'll explore the ways emotional intelligence plays out in these two crucial aspects of life.

EQ in Personal Relationships

Personal relationships—whether with family, friends, or romantic partners—are deeply influenced by how we manage and express our emotions. In my own life, the times I've struggled most in relationships were often when I was out of touch with my emotions, reacting impulsively or failing to understand the emotional needs of others.

As I began to develop emotional intelligence, I noticed significant improvements in how I connected with those around me. I realized that many conflicts arise not from the actual issue at hand but from misunderstandings of emotional signals. For example, in one of my closest relationships, a simple disagreement about plans would escalate because neither of us was really tuned in to what the other was feeling. Once I learned to pause, reflect on my emotions, and ask how the other person was feeling, our conflicts became less heated and more constructive.

Managing Conflicts with EQ

When you approach conflicts with emotional intelligence, you're better equipped to manage them in a calm and balanced way. I've found that instead of reacting defensively, I'm able to step back and recognize both my emotional triggers and the underlying emotions of the other person. This has been a game-changer in resolving disagreements. It's not about winning the argument, but about understanding where each person is coming from emotionally.

For example, there was a time when a close friend and I were constantly butting heads. I used to see our disagreements as a sign that we were drifting apart, but once I started applying EQ, I realized our conflicts were often fueled by underlying stress and unspoken frustrations. I learned to ask questions like, "What's really going on here?" and "How can we both feel heard?" This shifted our dynamic from confrontation to collaboration.

Improving Communication

EQ also plays a significant role in improving communication, which is the bedrock of any healthy relationship. In my early years, I struggled with being overly reactive in conversations, especially when I felt misunderstood. As I worked on my emotional intelligence, I became more mindful of how I expressed myself and how I listened to others.

I remember a pivotal moment when I had a disagreement with a family member. Instead of jumping to conclusions or letting my emotions take control, I paused and focused on what they were saying. I allowed myself to really listen—not just to their words, but to the emotions behind them. This small change transformed the conversation. Instead of escalating, we found common ground, and the relationship grew stronger because I was able to communicate more empathetically and effectively.

Emotional intelligence teaches us that communication isn't just about talking; it's about listening with empathy and responding thoughtfully. The more I practiced this, the deeper my relationships became.

Building Stronger, Empathetic Relationships

Empathy is one of the most powerful components of emotional intelligence, and it's essential for building lasting relationships. When I began actively trying to understand what others were feeling, even when they didn't explicitly say it, my connections with people transformed.

There was a time when a close friend was going through a rough period, and although they didn't openly share their struggles, I could sense something was off. Instead of pressing them for details, I simply offered support and let them know I was there if they needed to talk. In time, they opened up, and our relationship became even stronger. It was my growing empathy that allowed me to be a source of comfort during that difficult time.

EQ in the Workplace

Just as emotional intelligence strengthens personal relationships, it is equally vital in the workplace. In fact, as I advanced in my career, I realized that EQ was often more important than technical skills when it came to navigating workplace dynamics and achieving long-term success.

Leadership and EQ

In leadership, emotional intelligence is not just an asset—it's a necessity. I've observed that leaders with high EQ are far more effective at inspiring their teams, resolving conflicts, and fostering a positive work culture. Early in my career, I worked under a manager who embodied emotional intelligence. He wasn't just focused on results; he was deeply attuned to how each member of the team was feeling. He would check in with us regularly, not only about work but about our personal well-being.

This approach created an atmosphere of trust and openness, where everyone felt valued and understood. I realized that emotional intelligence in leadership goes beyond decision-making; it's about building an environment where people feel supported and motivated to perform at their best.

When I began leading teams, I made it a priority to cultivate these same skills. I noticed that when I was emotionally present with my team, the results spoke for themselves—people were more engaged, morale was higher, and collaboration came naturally. It reinforced to me that EQ is a vital component of effective leadership.

Teamwork and Collaboration

EQ also plays a crucial role in teamwork. I've worked on projects where emotional intelligence made all the difference between success and failure. In high-pressure situations, emotions can run high, and without emotional intelligence, teams can quickly spiral into conflict or disengagement.

However, when team members have strong emotional intelligence, they are more likely to manage stress effectively, communicate openly, and work together toward a common goal. I've found that fostering emotional awareness within teams leads to better collaboration, as people are more willing to listen, compromise, and respect each other's perspectives.

Decision-Making and Job Performance

In my experience, EQ has also been key in making better decisions, both personally and professionally. When I'm emotionally aware, I make more thoughtful, balanced choices, even in stressful situations. Instead of letting anxiety or frustration dictate my decisions, I'm able to take a step back, assess the situation objectively, and make decisions that are aligned with my values and long-term goals.

In the workplace, this ability to manage emotions under pressure is invaluable. Whether it's meeting tight deadlines, handling client expectations, or navigating office politics, EQ helps me stay calm, focused, and productive. It's a skill that has enhanced not only my job performance but also my job satisfaction.

With emotional intelligence at the forefront of both personal and professional relationships, it's clear that EQ is the key to building meaningful connections, fostering collaboration, and achieving long-term success. In the next chapter, we'll explore practical strategies for **developing emotional intelligence** and how you can apply these skills in your everyday life.

Chapter 3: Developing Self-Awareness

Self-awareness is the cornerstone of emotional intelligence. It's the starting point for understanding how our emotions influence our thoughts, behaviors, and interactions. Before we can effectively manage our emotions or empathize with others, we need to cultivate a deeper understanding of ourselves. In this chapter, we'll explore the steps to develop self-awareness, beginning with understanding our emotions, recognizing emotional triggers, and building emotional insight.

Understanding Your Emotions

One of the first steps in developing emotional intelligence is gaining a clearer understanding of your emotions. In my own experience, I've found that many of us go through life on emotional autopilot—reacting to situations without pausing to reflect on why we feel the way we do. I was guilty of this for years. When stress hit, I would automatically shift into overdrive, pushing myself harder rather than stepping back and acknowledging my feelings. Success often came with a sense of relief, but I seldom stopped to celebrate or even understand the emotions that accompanied it. Failure would hit me like a ton of bricks, but instead of dissecting those feelings, I'd simply try to push through them.

It wasn't until I began to focus on self-awareness that I realized how little I truly understood my emotions. This shift began with a simple but powerful practice—reflection. I started journaling, a habit that gave me the space to process my thoughts and emotions without judgment. When I faced a challenge at work or a conflict in a relationship, I wrote about how I felt—what specific emotions were arising and how they influenced my thoughts and actions.

Journaling became my emotional mirror. It allowed me to notice patterns in my responses to different situations. For example, I realized that whenever I faced criticism, I immediately felt defensive. But instead of simply feeling the emotion and moving on, I began to ask myself why. Where was this defensiveness coming from? Was it a fear of failure or a lack of confidence in that particular area?

This process helped me recognize that my emotions were signals, not obstacles. They were telling me something about my deeper beliefs and experiences. By understanding them, I could begin to manage them more effectively.

Practical Exercise: Journaling for Emotional Awareness

I recommend setting aside a few minutes each day to reflect on your emotions. You can do this at the end of the day or right after a particularly emotional experience. Write about how you felt during the day, what triggered those emotions, and how you responded. Over time, you'll start to see patterns in your emotional reactions, and this awareness will be the first step in managing them more constructively.

Using Mindfulness to Increase Self-Awareness

Another technique that helped me develop emotional awareness is mindfulness. Mindfulness is the practice of being fully present in the moment, without judgment. I initially struggled with mindfulness because my mind was always racing. But as I began to practice it more regularly, I found it incredibly powerful for tuning into my emotions.

Mindfulness allowed me to catch my emotions as they arose, rather than letting them simmer beneath the surface. For example, during a stressful workday, I would notice my anxiety building up. Instead of ignoring it, I would take a few deep breaths, center myself, and acknowledge the emotion. By being present with my feelings, I could manage them before they spiraled out of control.

Incorporating mindfulness into your daily routine, even for just a few minutes, can help you become more in tune with your emotional landscape. The more aware you are of your emotions in the moment, the better you'll be at handling them with clarity and purpose.

Recognizing Emotional Triggers

Self-awareness goes beyond just understanding our emotions; it also requires us to recognize the situations, people, or environments that consistently trigger strong emotional reactions. Emotional triggers are often deeply rooted in past experiences or unresolved issues, and they can significantly impact our behavior if left unchecked. I've had to learn this the hard way in my own journey toward emotional intelligence.

There was a period in my life when certain situations would set me off almost instantly. I'd find myself getting frustrated or anxious without really understanding why. It wasn't until I started digging deeper that I discovered these reactions were connected to emotional triggers I wasn't fully aware of. For example, criticism from a colleague would immediately make me feel defensive, even if the feedback was constructive. It wasn't the words themselves but a long-standing sensitivity to judgment that had its roots in my childhood experiences of trying to meet high expectations.

Identifying Your Emotional Triggers

The key to managing emotional triggers is first identifying them. This process requires reflection and honesty. What are the specific situations that cause you to react strongly? Do certain people or behaviors irritate you more than others? Are there themes in your reactions—perhaps around control, recognition, or feeling misunderstood?

I found it helpful to keep track of these triggers in my journal. Each time I felt an emotional reaction that seemed disproportionate to the situation, I would note it down. Over time, a pattern began to emerge. I discovered that my defensiveness was triggered not by criticism itself but by how it was delivered—if I felt it questioned my competence, I would react more intensely. I also realized that I was particularly sensitive to interruptions when I was deep in thought, which would trigger frustration.

The Role of Past Experiences

Emotional triggers are often linked to past experiences, sometimes even from childhood. For example, someone who grew up in an environment where they felt overlooked or unappreciated may find themselves triggered when they perceive they aren't being acknowledged. Recognizing this connection to the past can help you better understand your current emotional landscape.

In my case, the defensiveness I experienced in response to criticism stemmed from a need for validation and perfectionism that had been ingrained in me from an early age. Once I made this connection, I could start addressing the underlying issue rather than just reacting emotionally in the moment.

Managing Emotional Triggers

Once you've identified your triggers, the next step is learning to manage them. This doesn't mean suppressing your emotions but rather acknowledging them and finding healthier ways to respond. One technique I've found helpful is what I call the "pause and process" method. Whenever I feel triggered, I take a mental step back and ask myself a few key questions:

1. **What emotion am I feeling right now?**
2. **Why am I feeling this way?**
3. **Is my reaction proportional to the situation?**
4. **What is a more constructive way to respond?**

This pause gives me time to process the emotion before it escalates into a reaction I might regret. In some cases, I've found that simply taking a few deep breaths or stepping away from the situation for a moment helps me regain control over my emotions.

Turning Triggers into Growth Opportunities

One of the most powerful lessons I've learned is that emotional triggers can be opportunities for growth. Every time we encounter a trigger, we have a chance to practice emotional regulation and become more resilient. Instead of viewing triggers as obstacles, we can view them as invitations to deepen our self-awareness and develop healthier emotional responses.

By recognizing and managing your triggers, you'll not only improve your emotional intelligence but also build stronger, more stable relationships with others. You'll be less likely to react impulsively or defensively and more able to approach situations with clarity and calm.

Building Emotional Insight

Self-awareness is only the first step in developing emotional intelligence. Once you understand your emotions and recognize your triggers, the next stage is to deepen that awareness into what I call "emotional insight." This involves gaining a deeper understanding of the patterns, motivations, and beliefs that influence your emotional world. Developing emotional insight helps you not only respond more effectively to situations but also grow as an individual.

When I started my journey to emotional intelligence, I realized that simply being aware of my emotions wasn't enough. I needed to understand *why* I felt the way I did in certain situations and *what* those emotions were trying to tell me. This process of cultivating emotional insight was eye-opening and, at times, difficult, but it helped me become more in tune with my emotional landscape and, in turn, more at peace with myself.

Deepening Emotional Insight through Reflection

The first step to building emotional insight is regular reflection. While self-awareness involves understanding how you feel in the moment, emotional insight is about analyzing those emotions after the fact, looking for patterns or deeper truths. One of the most effective tools I've found for this is journaling.

Each day, I take a few minutes to write about the most significant emotional experiences I had that day. I ask myself questions like:
- **What was the strongest emotion I felt today?**
- **What triggered that emotion?**
- **What thoughts or beliefs were behind that emotion?**
- **How did I react, and how could I have reacted better?**

This practice helps me to look beyond the surface level of my emotions and dig deeper into the underlying reasons for them. Over time, I began to notice recurring themes. For instance, I realized that my frustration with a co-worker's comments was more about my fear of inadequacy than the actual content of the conversation. By reflecting on these experiences, I gained clarity on how my past and beliefs were shaping my emotional responses.

Meditation and Mindfulness for Emotional Insight

Another powerful practice that has helped me develop emotional insight is meditation. Through mindfulness, I learned to observe my emotions without judgment or the need to immediately react. This gave me the space to understand them better.

When I meditate, I focus on bringing my awareness to the present moment, whether I'm focusing on my breath or a simple mantra. In doing so, I've noticed that emotions naturally rise to the surface. By allowing myself to sit with these emotions without pushing them away or acting on them, I started to understand their nature. Meditation helped me realize that emotions, like all thoughts, are transient—they come and go, and we don't always have to be controlled by them.

This practice taught me that my emotions were not as overwhelming as they sometimes felt. By simply observing them, I could gain distance from them, allowing me to analyze and understand them more deeply.

Seeking Feedback for Greater Insight

While self-reflection and meditation are valuable tools, one of the most effective ways I've found to build emotional insight is by seeking honest feedback from others. It's one thing to understand how you perceive your emotions, but it's another to understand how others perceive your emotional responses.

Early in my career, I had a mentor who was direct but compassionate in offering feedback. One day, after a particularly stressful meeting, I asked for feedback on how I had handled myself. She pointed out that while I had stayed composed, my body language and tone had conveyed frustration and defensiveness, even though I had tried hard to mask those feelings. This was a revelation for me—I hadn't realized how much my internal emotions were being communicated nonverbally.

That experience taught me the importance of seeking feedback from people I trust. Their perspectives often reveal emotional blind spots we may not notice ourselves. Since then, I've made it a habit to periodically ask for feedback from close friends, colleagues, and family members. Their insights have helped me adjust my behavior and emotional responses in ways I couldn't have done on my own.

Embracing Vulnerability for Emotional Growth

One of the final keys to building emotional insight is embracing vulnerability. Often, our deepest emotional insights come from our most vulnerable moments—the times when we feel exposed, unsure, or even afraid. For many years, I resisted vulnerability because I saw it as a weakness. But as I've grown emotionally, I've come to realize that vulnerability is actually a strength. It's in those moments of vulnerability that we learn the most about ourselves.

I remember a time when I was struggling with a personal relationship, and I tried to keep my emotions in check to avoid appearing weak. But when I finally allowed myself to be vulnerable—to admit my insecurities and fears—I not only gained deeper insight into my own emotional patterns but also strengthened the relationship. Being open and honest about my feelings helped me build a deeper connection with the other person and, more importantly, with myself.

Emotional insight is about going beyond surface-level awareness. It's about examining your emotions closely, reflecting on their origins, and being open to feedback and vulnerability. By cultivating emotional insight, you gain the tools to not only understand your emotions but also harness them in a way that enhances your relationships, your decision-making, and your overall well-being.

Chapter 4: Cultivating Emotional Control

One of the most important skills in developing emotional intelligence is learning how to control our emotional responses. Emotional control isn't about suppressing your feelings, but rather managing how and when you express them. I've found that cultivating emotional control helps not only in moments of stress but also in everyday interactions, allowing me to approach life's challenges with a sense of calm and clarity.

The Power of Pause

In my journey to becoming more emotionally intelligent, one of the most valuable lessons I've learned is the importance of pausing. Reacting impulsively to emotions can often lead to regrettable outcomes—saying something in anger, making hasty decisions, or simply allowing emotions to cloud judgment. The power of pause is about giving yourself a moment to step back before you react, creating a space where you can choose your response instead of being driven by immediate emotion.

When I first started practicing this, I would find myself in heated conversations, wanting to jump in and defend my point of view or express my frustration. But over time, I realized that those were the moments when a pause was most needed. Pausing doesn't have to be long; it can be as brief as taking a deep breath or counting to three. This simple act allows your brain to shift out of an emotional hijack and into a state where you can think more clearly.

In those moments of pause, I ask myself:
- **What am I really feeling right now?**
- **What do I want to achieve with my response?**
- **How will my reaction impact the situation or the people involved?**

This small act of reflection often helps me choose a more thoughtful, measured response. In the past, I might have said something sharp or defensive in an argument. But now, with the power of pause, I find myself more likely to ask a question or clarify my understanding, which leads to a more productive and less emotionally charged conversation.

The Pause in High-Stress Situations

The power of pause isn't just useful in personal conversations; it's also incredibly valuable in high-stress situations. I remember a time when I was leading a project at work, and things weren't going according to plan. Tensions were high, deadlines were approaching, and emotions were running wild. In the past, I would have let the stress get to me, probably snapping at my team or allowing panic to drive my decisions. But during this particular project, I had committed to using the pause as a tool for emotional control.

During one particularly challenging meeting, where everyone seemed overwhelmed, I felt the familiar rise of stress and frustration. My natural impulse was to jump in and assert control, but instead, I took a pause. I took a slow, deep breath, reminding myself that reacting emotionally wouldn't solve the problem. That brief pause allowed me to approach the situation with calmness and clarity, offering a solution that diffused the tension and kept the team moving forward.

Pausing before reacting doesn't eliminate stress or difficult emotions, but it gives you the power to manage them in a way that helps rather than hinders. It's a way to ground yourself and regain control in moments when emotions threaten to take over.

Pausing Before Important Decisions

Another place where the power of pause has had a profound effect on my life is in decision-making. We all face moments where our emotions—whether excitement, fear, or anxiety—can lead us to make decisions that we later regret. Pausing before making important decisions has saved me from countless mistakes.

One of the techniques I've adopted is the "**24-hour rule**." When faced with an important decision, especially one that elicits a strong emotional reaction, I wait 24 hours before finalizing my choice. Whether it's making a significant financial decision or responding to an emotional email, giving myself this time allows the intensity of my emotions to subside so that I can approach the decision more logically.

I've found that when I act too quickly, especially when emotions are high, I often miss critical details or fail to consider the long-term consequences. The pause creates space for rational thinking, ensuring that I make decisions that align with my values and long-term goals.

Managing Stress and Anxiety

Stress and anxiety are inevitable parts of life, but how we manage them can make all the difference in maintaining emotional control. Over the years, I've come to realize that emotional intelligence doesn't mean avoiding stress but knowing how to navigate through it without letting it overwhelm you. When stress and anxiety build up, they can easily cloud your judgment and trigger emotional responses that don't serve you. Learning how to manage these emotions effectively is key to staying composed, even when life feels chaotic.

The Impact of Stress on Emotions

In my experience, stress manifests in different ways for different people. For some, it's the physical symptoms: tense shoulders, headaches, or difficulty sleeping. For others, it's emotional—feeling overwhelmed, irritable, or on the verge of tears. I've dealt with both, and I've seen how stress, when left unmanaged, can lead to emotional outbursts or a complete shutdown of communication. These reactions aren't a true reflection of who we are but are our emotions taking control of us.

Recognizing when stress is building is the first step in managing it. I've found that becoming aware of my body's stress signals—tight muscles, shallow breathing, or racing thoughts—helps me catch stress before it spirals. Once I'm aware, I can choose to address it with practical tools that calm my mind and body, rather than letting it fester until it bursts out uncontrollably.

Breathing Techniques for Instant Calm

One of the most effective tools I've learned for managing stress is conscious breathing. It sounds almost too simple, but the way we breathe has a direct impact on how we feel. When stress or anxiety hits, our breathing becomes shallow and rapid, which only increases feelings of tension. By focusing on deep, controlled breathing, we can reverse this process and calm both the body and mind.

One breathing exercise that has worked wonders for me is the **4-7-8 technique**:
- **Inhale** for 4 seconds through your nose.
- **Hold** the breath for 7 seconds.
- **Exhale** slowly for 8 seconds through your mouth.

This technique helps to slow down your heart rate and lower anxiety levels almost instantly. I use it in moments of high stress—before a difficult conversation, during a hectic workday, or when I feel anxiety creeping in. It only takes a minute or two, but it helps bring me back to a state of calm where I can think more clearly and control my emotions better.

Healthy Outlets for Stress

Another key aspect of managing stress is having healthy outlets. I've learned that bottling up emotions doesn't work in the long run. Stress needs to be released in healthy ways, or it will come out at inopportune moments. For me, physical exercise has always been one of the best ways to release built-up tension. Whether it's going for a run, practicing yoga, or simply taking a brisk walk, moving my body helps me process stress and release it.

Along with exercise, I've found journaling to be another effective way to manage stress. Writing down what I'm feeling—without judgment—gives me a space to process my emotions and make sense of what's going on inside. Sometimes, seeing the words on the page helps me understand the root of my stress and come up with practical solutions, rather than letting the emotions control me.

The Role of Routine in Managing Stress

I've also discovered that having a daily routine can be a powerful way to manage stress and maintain emotional control. When life feels chaotic, a routine creates a sense of order and stability. For me, sticking to a morning routine—waking up at the same time, practicing mindfulness, and planning my day—helps me start the day from a place of calm, rather than rushing into the day's stressors. Similarly, ending the day with a wind-down routine—whether it's reading, reflecting, or meditating—helps me release any residual stress and prepare for a restful night's sleep.

By integrating these small but consistent practices into my life, I've found that I'm much better equipped to handle stress when it arises. The key is not to wait until stress is overwhelming but to have strategies in place that prevent it from getting to that point.

Stress and anxiety are natural parts of life, but they don't have to control us. By learning how to manage these emotions, we can stay grounded and maintain emotional control, even in the most challenging situations.

Practicing Emotional Regulation

Emotional regulation is the ability to manage your emotions effectively, especially in challenging or stressful situations. Over the years, I've come to understand that mastering emotional regulation is not about suppressing emotions but rather learning to respond to them in a way that aligns with my values and goals. In many instances, emotional regulation has helped me navigate tough conversations, maintain composure under pressure, and make decisions based on logic rather than impulsive reactions.

Recognizing the Importance of Regulation

When emotions run high, it's easy to let them dictate our actions. I've been there—feeling frustrated, anxious, or even angry—and reacting in ways that I later regretted. In those moments, the emotions I was feeling were legitimate, but the way I responded to them was not always helpful. That's why practicing emotional regulation has been so important in my life.

The key is learning how to pause and process emotions before reacting. Whether it's anger, frustration, or sadness, all emotions carry information, but acting on them without thinking can lead to consequences that don't serve our long-term interests. Emotional regulation helps us create that pause, allowing us to respond rather than react.

Techniques for Emotional Regulation

One of the first steps to regulating emotions is **labeling** them. When I feel overwhelmed, simply identifying what I'm experiencing—whether it's frustration, disappointment, or stress—helps me begin the process of regulation. It's like shining a light on the emotion, giving it a name, and allowing myself to understand it better. Labeling has given me the ability to separate myself from the emotion, which makes it easier to manage.

I also rely on **reframing**, a cognitive technique where I change the way I perceive a situation to shift my emotional response. For example, when I feel frustrated because of a setback, instead of viewing it as a failure, I try to reframe it as a learning opportunity. This shift in perspective doesn't erase the frustration but makes it more manageable and less overwhelming.

Another technique that has proven effective is **grounding**. When emotions start to spiral out of control, I use grounding exercises—such as focusing on my breath, feeling my feet firmly on the ground, or noticing my surroundings—to bring myself back to the present moment. Grounding helps me center myself and regain control over how I'm feeling, rather than being swept away by emotions.

Regulating Emotions in the Workplace

In professional settings, emotional regulation becomes especially important. I've found that the workplace is often a breeding ground for stress, and without strong emotional regulation skills, it's easy to react impulsively or let emotions affect performance. Whether it's dealing with a difficult colleague, managing a tight deadline, or receiving critical feedback, emotions can flare up. However, staying composed and responding thoughtfully has helped me navigate these situations with grace.

One strategy that's been particularly useful in the workplace is **taking a step back**—both literally and figuratively. If I find myself getting overwhelmed or upset, I take a few moments to step away from the situation, clear my head, and return with a more measured response. This simple act of creating space allows emotions to settle and prevents knee-jerk reactions that might escalate the situation.

Real-Time Emotional Control

There have been countless moments when I've had to regulate my emotions in real-time—whether in a tense meeting, a disagreement with a loved one, or a stressful situation. One technique that's helped me immensely is **counting to ten** before responding. This pause gives me the time to assess the situation and choose how to respond rather than reacting impulsively. It's amazing how such a small act can make such a big difference.

I've also learned to **focus on my body's cues** during emotional moments. When I feel anger or frustration rising, I notice my heart rate speeding up, my muscles tensing, or my breathing becoming shallow. Recognizing these physical signals is often a clue that I need to calm down before continuing the conversation. Taking slow, deep breaths or even briefly excusing myself from the situation allows me to regain emotional control.

Why Emotional Regulation Matters

Practicing emotional regulation has made a significant difference in both my personal and professional life. It's given me the ability to face challenges without being derailed by my emotions and to handle conflicts with calmness and clarity. Emotional regulation doesn't mean suppressing or ignoring emotions; it means recognizing them, understanding them, and making a conscious choice about how to respond.

By incorporating these practices into my life, I've become more resilient, more empathetic, and better equipped to handle whatever comes my way. Emotional regulation is an ongoing process, but with time and practice, it becomes a natural part of how you navigate the world.

Chapter 5: Enhancing Empathy

Empathy is one of the most transformative skills anyone can develop. It has allowed me to build deeper connections, foster trust, and resolve conflicts more effectively in both my personal and professional life. In this chapter, I will share how empathy works in practice and how you, too, can nurture and enhance this vital part of emotional intelligence.

Active Listening

When I first started paying attention to how I communicated with others, I realized that, more often than not, I wasn't really **listening**—I was simply waiting for my turn to speak. It was eye-opening to recognize how much I missed by not being fully present in conversations. Active listening, as I've learned, is the key to true empathy. It's not just about hearing the words spoken; it's about understanding the emotions and intentions behind them.

Active listening means giving someone your undivided attention. We live in a world full of distractions—our phones, emails, and to-do lists constantly vying for our focus. But when someone is speaking to you, it's essential to be fully present. This isn't easy, but it's worth the effort. When I began to consciously listen to people without thinking of my response or getting distracted by other thoughts, I noticed an immediate change in the quality of my conversations. People felt heard, and that created a deeper level of trust.

How to Listen Actively

Active listening starts with **eye contact**. It's such a simple gesture, but it makes a big difference. When I maintain eye contact with someone, I'm signaling that I'm fully engaged and interested in what they have to say. It creates a bond of trust and helps me focus on the conversation rather than letting my mind wander.

Another key to active listening is **asking clarifying questions**. If someone shares something, rather than jumping in with my own thoughts or advice, I've learned to ask questions that help me understand their point of view better. For example, if a friend is telling me about a difficult situation at work, instead of immediately offering solutions, I might ask, "How did that make you feel?" or "What do you think could help in this situation?" These types of questions show that I'm not just listening passively but truly trying to understand their emotions and perspective.

I also pay close attention to **non-verbal cues**—not just the words being spoken, but the tone, body language, and facial expressions that accompany them. Sometimes, what someone is saying on the surface doesn't match how they're feeling underneath. I've been in conversations where a person is saying they're "fine," but their body language or tone suggests otherwise. By tuning into these subtle cues, I can better understand what's really going on and respond more empathetically.

Avoiding Distractions

One of the hardest parts of active listening is staying present and avoiding distractions. In our fast-paced world, multitasking has become a norm, but it's the enemy of true listening. I've been guilty of trying to hold conversations while checking my phone or glancing at emails, but I quickly realized that this undermines the quality of the interaction. Now, when I'm engaging in an important conversation, I make a conscious effort to put my phone away, close my laptop, and focus entirely on the person in front of me.

When I'm fully engaged in listening, I find that people are more open and honest with me. They feel respected and valued, and in turn, I can understand them on a deeper level. This has improved my relationships immensely, both personally and professionally.

The Impact of Active Listening

Through active listening, I've been able to resolve conflicts more effectively. When someone feels heard, they're less likely to be defensive or aggressive. I've found that even in heated conversations, simply letting the other person express themselves without interruption can diffuse tension. Once they've had the chance to fully express their thoughts and feelings, I'm in a better position to respond thoughtfully, rather than reacting impulsively.

In professional settings, active listening has helped me foster stronger connections with colleagues and clients. It shows that I value their input and respect their opinions, which in turn, builds trust and collaboration. People are much more willing to work with you when they feel understood, and active listening is the foundation of that understanding.

In summary, active listening is a skill that anyone can develop with practice. It takes patience and effort, but the rewards are profound. By being fully present, asking thoughtful questions, and paying attention to non-verbal cues, you can create deeper, more meaningful connections with those around you.

Perspective-Taking

Empathy is more than just hearing someone's words—it's about seeing the world through their eyes. In my journey of developing emotional intelligence, I found that perspective-taking transformed how I connect with others. It helped me step out of my own mindset and consider the emotions, thoughts, and motivations of those around me.

Why Perspective-Taking Matters

When I began practicing perspective-taking, I realized how limited my understanding of others had been. Often, I would react to situations based on my own experiences, assumptions, and biases without fully considering where the other person was coming from. This led to misunderstandings and, at times, unnecessary conflict. Perspective-taking, however, allowed me to see beyond my initial judgments. I began to ask myself:
- **What might this person be going through?**
- **What fears, desires, or pressures are influencing their behavior?**

This practice has been especially helpful in difficult situations. For example, during a disagreement, instead of jumping to conclusions or becoming defensive, I now take a moment to imagine how the other person is feeling. It's not always easy, especially in heated moments, but I've found that pausing and asking, **What is their point of view?** helps me stay calm and approach the conversation with empathy.

In both personal and professional relationships, taking someone else's perspective fosters understanding and reduces conflict. When I started seeing things from another's viewpoint, I began to notice that people felt more comfortable opening up to me. They sensed that I wasn't just reacting based on my own emotions, but truly trying to understand theirs.

How to Practice Perspective-Taking

One of the most valuable tools I've used to improve perspective-taking is **self-reflection**. After a conversation or interaction, I take a few moments to reflect on how I responded and consider how the other person may have felt. Did I overlook their perspective? Did I react based on assumptions? Over time, this reflection has helped me become more mindful of how I approach interactions in real-time.

Another method that has helped me is asking **open-ended questions**. When someone shares their feelings or thoughts, instead of assuming I know what they mean, I ask questions like: **Can you help me understand what you're feeling?** or **What do you need right now?** These questions not only clarify their perspective but also show that I genuinely care about understanding them.

I've also found that reading books or watching films that challenge my worldview can improve my ability to take others' perspectives. Stories—whether fictional or real—offer insights into lives and experiences vastly different from our own. By immersing myself in diverse narratives, I've broadened my understanding of the human experience, which, in turn, deepens my empathy in real-life interactions.

Overcoming Biases and Assumptions

One of the challenges I've faced in perspective-taking is overcoming my own biases. We all have preconceived notions based on our upbringing, culture, and personal experiences, and these can cloud our ability to see things from another's perspective. For example, I used to assume that people who responded negatively in stressful situations were simply being difficult. However, through practicing perspective-taking, I started to realize that their reactions often stemmed from deeper issues, such as personal stress or fear.

Recognizing my own biases has been a humbling process. I now approach conversations with an open mind, reminding myself that my perspective is just one version of the story. This shift has allowed me to navigate conflicts with greater ease, as I'm less focused on proving myself right and more focused on understanding the full picture.

The Benefits of Perspective-Taking

The practice of perspective-taking has enriched my relationships in ways I hadn't imagined. I've become more patient, less judgmental, and more willing to work through differences. Whether I'm dealing with a loved one, a colleague, or even a stranger, taking the time to understand their point of view leads to more compassionate and effective communication.

In professional settings, perspective-taking has made me a better leader and collaborator. By considering the viewpoints of my team members or clients, I can address their concerns more thoughtfully, leading to stronger relationships and more productive outcomes.

Overall, perspective-taking is an invaluable tool for deepening empathy. It allows us to move beyond our own limitations, opening us to the richness of others' experiences. Through this practice, we can create more meaningful, supportive, and understanding relationships in all areas of life.

Cultivating Compassion

Compassion, for me, is the heart of emotional intelligence. It goes beyond understanding or sympathizing with someone's feelings—compassion is about actively wanting to alleviate someone's suffering or discomfort. In my experience, developing compassion has been a transformative journey that has deepened my connections with others and enriched my emotional life.

What is Compassion?

At its core, compassion is the desire to help others. It means we care deeply enough about someone's struggles that we are moved to take action, whether that's offering support, lending a listening ear, or simply being present in their time of need. Compassion, I've learned, is not about fixing people's problems, but about offering understanding and kindness, without judgment.

In the past, I often felt overwhelmed when people I cared about were going through difficult times. I'd think, **How can I help? What can I do to make things better for them?** But over time, I realized that compassion isn't about having all the answers. It's about showing up, being there, and offering genuine care without trying to take control of their situation.

How Compassion Enhances Relationships

One of the most powerful lessons I've learned through cultivating compassion is that it can bridge even the widest emotional gaps. In moments of conflict, compassion allows us to look beyond our own hurt or frustration and recognize the humanity in the other person. It shifts our focus from being defensive or reactive to being caring and understanding.

For example, in personal relationships, I've found that when someone is angry or upset, responding with compassion changes the entire dynamic. Instead of reacting with anger or defensiveness, I take a moment to pause and think, **This person is hurting. How can I support them through this?** This mindset not only diffuses tension but also creates space for healing and resolution.

In my professional life, I've seen how compassion strengthens teams and fosters collaboration. When people feel that they are understood and supported, they are more willing to contribute their best efforts. As a leader, showing compassion toward colleagues—whether they're dealing with personal struggles or work-related challenges—has helped me build stronger, more trusting relationships.

Practicing Compassion in Everyday Life

Cultivating compassion isn't something that happens overnight—it's a daily practice. I've developed several habits that help me stay compassionate, even when I'm feeling stressed or overwhelmed.

First, I make a conscious effort to **slow down**. In our fast-paced world, it's easy to rush through interactions without truly connecting. By slowing down and being present in conversations, I've learned to listen more attentively and respond more thoughtfully. This simple shift allows me to show up fully for others, offering my undivided attention and care.

Second, I practice **self-compassion**. It's hard to extend compassion to others if we're constantly harsh or critical of ourselves. By learning to be kinder to myself—acknowledging my own struggles without judgment—I've become more empathetic and understanding toward others.

Lastly, I focus on **small acts of kindness**. Compassion doesn't always require grand gestures; it can be as simple as offering a kind word, checking in on someone, or lending a helping hand. These small acts may seem insignificant, but they often have a profound impact on the people we interact with.

Compassion as a Leadership Quality

One of the most unexpected places where I've seen compassion make a difference is in leadership. Early in my career, I believed that being a leader meant being strong, decisive, and focused solely on results. But over time, I've come to understand that true leadership involves compassion. When leaders show genuine concern for their team members' well-being, it creates a culture of trust, respect, and loyalty.

For instance, when a team member is struggling with a heavy workload or personal issue, a compassionate leader doesn't just focus on deadlines or productivity. Instead, they ask, **How can I support you?** This question, simple as it may be, acknowledges the person's humanity and helps them feel valued. In my own leadership roles, I've seen how this approach leads to not only happier, more engaged employees but also better outcomes for the team as a whole.

Compassion as a Path to Emotional Healing

Compassion also plays a vital role in emotional healing, both for ourselves and others. I've witnessed how offering compassion—whether to a friend going through grief or a colleague dealing with burnout—can provide comfort and a sense of relief. Compassion reminds people that they are not alone in their struggles and that they are seen and cared for.

In my own life, there have been times when I've felt emotionally drained or overwhelmed. During these moments, receiving compassion from others—whether through a kind word or a simple gesture—has been incredibly healing. It's a reminder that we don't have to carry our burdens alone and that there is always someone willing to offer support.

The Ripple Effect of Compassion

Compassion is contagious. When we act with compassion, it inspires others to do the same. I've seen this ripple effect in both personal and professional settings. A single act of kindness can set off a chain reaction, creating a more supportive and empathetic environment for everyone involved.

Whether we're offering compassion to a stranger, a loved one, or a colleague, the impact is profound. It not only strengthens relationships but also fosters a sense of connection and shared humanity.

In my journey of developing emotional intelligence, I've come to believe that compassion is one of the most powerful forces we can cultivate. It helps us navigate challenges with grace, build deeper relationships, and make a positive impact in the world around us.

Chapter 6: Building Stronger Relationships through EQ

Improving Communication

Communication is at the core of every relationship, whether personal or professional. Throughout my life, I've learned that how we communicate is often more important than what we communicate. Emotional intelligence has taught me that it's not just about saying the right words—it's about understanding the emotions behind those words and ensuring the other person feels heard, respected, and valued.

One of the key insights I've gained is that emotionally intelligent communication is built on three pillars: clarity, openness, and non-defensive responses. Mastering these can profoundly transform how we interact with others.

Clarity in Communication

In my early years, I struggled with vague communication. I'd assume people understood what I meant, only to find that misinterpretations would arise, leading to unnecessary misunderstandings. I realized that to build stronger relationships, I needed to be clear and direct about my thoughts, feelings, and needs. Emotional intelligence helped me understand that clear communication is about expressing myself in a way that leaves no room for ambiguity.

For example, rather than saying something like, **I'm fine**, when I was clearly upset, I learned to articulate my emotions more precisely. I'd say, **I'm feeling overwhelmed by the situation and need some time to process it.** This level of clarity helps others understand exactly what's going on with me, and it prevents them from guessing or making assumptions, which can lead to further confusion or frustration.

In conversations, I also make sure to clarify what the other person is saying. This has been a game-changer for me. Instead of assuming I understand their message, I ask, **Do you mean that...?** or **Let me make sure I understand what you're saying.** These small clarifications have gone a long way in improving communication and preventing misunderstandings.

Openness in Conversations

One of the most emotionally intelligent shifts I've made in my communication style is embracing openness. For years, I found myself holding back, unwilling to express my true thoughts or feelings in certain situations, especially when the topic was difficult or uncomfortable. This was because I feared judgment, rejection, or even conflict. But over time, I realized that genuine relationships are built on honesty and vulnerability.

Opening up and sharing my feelings has helped me connect with others on a deeper level. It's not just about sharing the good things but also being willing to express discomfort, disagreement, or hurt in a constructive way. When I approach conversations with openness, I've noticed others reciprocate with the same level of honesty, leading to more meaningful and authentic interactions.

Openness is also about being receptive to others' perspectives. It means creating a safe space where people feel comfortable expressing their thoughts without fear of judgment or dismissal. One thing that has worked for me is starting conversations with an open-ended question like, **How do you feel about this?** or **What's your perspective on this issue?**
These questions invite the other person to share openly and let me practice listening without rushing to judge or impose my opinions.

Non-Defensive Responses

This was one of the hardest communication skills for me to develop. In the past, if someone criticized or disagreed with me, I'd instinctively get defensive. I'd jump to explain or justify myself, which often escalated the situation rather than resolving it. Over time, emotional intelligence taught me that defensive reactions come from a place of insecurity or fear, and they close down the potential for genuine dialogue.

Now, when I feel criticized or misunderstood, I've learned to pause, take a breath, and respond with curiosity rather than defensiveness. Instead of thinking, **How can I prove I'm right?** I try to ask myself, **What can I learn from this perspective?** or **Is there truth in what they're saying?** This shift in mindset has made a huge difference. It allows me to stay calm, stay present, and keep the conversation constructive rather than adversarial.

One technique that's been incredibly helpful is simply acknowledging the other person's emotions. If someone says, **I'm frustrated because you didn't follow through on your commitment,** instead of jumping to my defense, I might respond, **I understand why you're frustrated, and I'm sorry for any inconvenience I caused**.
This simple acknowledgment defuses tension and opens the door for more productive communication.

In the end, emotionally intelligent communication isn't about never making mistakes—it's about being willing to acknowledge them, learn from them, and strive for better understanding and connection.

Conclusion: A New Approach to Communication

Incorporating emotional intelligence into communication doesn't happen overnight. It requires constant awareness, patience, and practice. But in my experience, the rewards are worth the effort. Clearer, more open, and non-defensive communication has not only improved my relationships but also helped me feel more connected and understood by the people around me.

Building these skills has allowed me to navigate difficult conversations with ease, resolve conflicts more effectively, and build deeper trust in all my relationships. For anyone looking to improve their emotional intelligence, I truly believe that communication is one of the most important areas to start.

Navigating Conflict with EQ

Conflict is an inevitable part of any relationship, whether personal or professional. How we handle it often determines the strength of the relationship moving forward. In the past, I saw conflict as something to be avoided at all costs, a mindset that led to unresolved tensions and misunderstandings. But as I grew in emotional intelligence, I realized that conflict, when approached constructively, can actually deepen relationships.

Emotional intelligence plays a crucial role in helping us navigate conflict in a way that preserves and strengthens relationships rather than damaging them. Here's how I've learned to approach conflict with emotional intelligence.

Staying Calm Under Pressure

One of the first things emotional intelligence taught me about conflict is the importance of remaining calm. I used to get caught up in the heat of the moment, letting my emotions—whether anger, frustration, or defensiveness—take control of the situation. More often than not, this led to saying things I didn't mean or escalating the situation further.

Now, I've learned to recognize when my emotions are getting the better of me. When I feel my heart rate rising or my thoughts racing, I take a moment to pause, breathe, and collect myself before responding. This simple act of pausing has made all the difference. It allows me to approach the situation from a place of composure rather than reacting impulsively.

In moments of conflict, I remind myself that staying calm doesn't mean ignoring my emotions or pretending they don't exist—it means acknowledging them without letting them control my actions. This emotional regulation is at the heart of conflict resolution.

Listening with Empathy

In emotionally charged situations, it's easy to focus only on our own perspective and feelings. In the past, I was quick to assume that I was in the right and the other person just didn't understand. But over time, I've come to see that listening with empathy is one of the most powerful tools in navigating conflict.

When someone expresses their frustration or disagreement, I make a conscious effort to listen deeply, not just to their words but to the emotions behind those words. This means putting aside my own need to be right and truly trying to understand where they're coming from. It's not about agreeing with them; it's about validating their feelings.

For instance, if a colleague comes to me with a complaint, instead of immediately defending my actions, I'll say something like, **I can see why this situation would be frustrating for you.** This simple acknowledgment of their emotions shows that I'm listening, and it helps to defuse the tension. People feel heard, which makes them more open to finding a resolution.

Focusing on Solutions, Not Blame

In the early days of my career, when conflict arose, I would often get stuck in the cycle of blame—either blaming myself or the other person. But over time, I've learned that focusing on blame rarely solves the problem. Emotional intelligence has taught me to shift my focus from assigning blame to finding solutions.

When a conflict arises, I try to approach it with a solution-oriented mindset. Instead of dwelling on what went wrong or who's at fault, I ask, **What can we do to resolve this?** This simple shift in focus keeps the conversation moving forward and helps both parties work together towards a resolution.

For example, in a disagreement with a partner or friend, I might say, **I understand that we're both feeling upset right now. How can we move forward in a way that works for both of us?** This approach opens the door to collaboration, where both people feel like they have a role in resolving the conflict, rather than being stuck in a cycle of blame.

Owning Your Part

Part of navigating conflict with emotional intelligence involves owning your role in the situation. It can be difficult to admit when we've contributed to a problem, but I've found that taking responsibility for my actions has been one of the most effective ways to resolve conflict.

When I've made a mistake or acted in a way that hurt someone, I've learned to own up to it without excuses. Saying something as simple as, **I realize that I was wrong in how I handled that,** or **I'm sorry for how my actions affected you,** goes a long way in rebuilding trust and opening the door to resolution.

Taking responsibility not only shows emotional maturity but also encourages the other person to do the same, creating a more balanced and constructive dialogue.

Finding Common Ground

In any conflict, it's important to find areas where both parties can agree. Emotional intelligence helps us move past the surface-level disagreements to identify common values, goals, or needs. This creates a foundation for resolving the conflict in a way that satisfies both parties.

For example, in a workplace conflict over a project's direction, I might say, *We both want this project to succeed, so how can we collaborate to make that happen?* This reaffirms that, despite our differences, we're on the same team. Identifying common ground shifts the focus from what divides us to what unites us, making it easier to find a resolution.

Conclusion: Turning Conflict into Connection

Navigating conflict with emotional intelligence has been one of the most transformative skills I've learned. Rather than seeing conflict as something to fear or avoid, I now view it as an opportunity to strengthen relationships and deepen understanding. By staying calm, listening with empathy, focusing on solutions, taking responsibility, and finding common ground, I've been able to turn conflicts into moments of growth and connection.

For anyone struggling with conflict, I encourage you to see it as an opportunity to practice emotional intelligence. With time and patience, you'll find that conflict, when handled with EQ, can actually bring people closer together rather than pushing them apart.

Developing Social Awareness

Social awareness is one of the key pillars of emotional intelligence, and it has been a game-changer in how I relate to the people around me. It's the ability to understand and respond to the emotions of others, not just in one-on-one interactions, but within groups and social settings as well. This section will explore how developing social awareness can lead to stronger, more meaningful connections, both personally and professionally.

Understanding Group Dynamics

One of the biggest revelations for me in developing social awareness was learning to read the dynamics in group settings. In the past, I would often be too focused on my own ideas and contributions, missing out on the subtle social cues that could tell me how the group was feeling or what the unspoken tensions were. Developing social awareness has helped me become more attuned to these undercurrents.

In a professional setting, for example, I started paying attention to how others react to certain topics, who tends to dominate the conversation, and who might be feeling left out. I realized that just because someone isn't speaking up, it doesn't mean they're disengaged; they might simply need encouragement to share their thoughts.

By becoming more aware of these dynamics, I've learned how to create space for everyone to contribute. I'll often say something like, *I noticed we haven't heard from Sarah yet—what are your thoughts?* This simple acknowledgment can make a huge difference, not only in ensuring all voices are heard but also in fostering a more inclusive environment.

Reading Non-Verbal Cues

Much of communication happens non-verbally, through body language, facial expressions, and tone of voice. Before developing social awareness, I was often too caught up in the content of what was being said to notice these critical cues. But over time, I've learned that paying attention to non-verbal communication can give you deep insights into what someone is truly feeling.

For example, if someone says they're fine but their arms are crossed and their tone is clipped, that's usually a sign that something is bothering them. I've learned to gently probe in these situations, saying something like, **I'm sensing that something might be off—do you want to talk about it?** Often, this opens the door for more honest communication and helps address any underlying issues before they escalate.

Reading non-verbal cues has also helped me become more empathetic. When I notice someone looking uncomfortable or stressed, even if they haven't said anything, I make a point to check in with them privately, offering support or asking if there's anything they need. This awareness has strengthened my relationships and made me a more compassionate leader and friend.

Building Rapport and Connection

At the heart of social awareness is the ability to build rapport and foster genuine connections with others. In my own journey, I found that developing this skill made a significant difference in both my personal and professional relationships.

Building rapport doesn't happen by accident—it requires intentionality. I started making a conscious effort to remember small details about people, such as their interests, family members, or recent life events. These small gestures, like asking about someone's recent vacation or congratulating them on a personal milestone, show that you care about them as a person, not just in a transactional way.

I also began practicing more openness in my interactions, sharing a bit about my own experiences to create a sense of mutual trust and vulnerability. This kind of sharing often leads to deeper conversations, allowing relationships to move beyond surface-level interactions. Whether it's in the workplace, with friends, or with family, building rapport creates a foundation for stronger, more meaningful connections.

Navigating Social Situations with Empathy

Social awareness also involves understanding the broader social context and how people might be feeling in various situations. For example, if I'm at a social event and notice someone standing alone or seeming uncomfortable, I'll make an effort to approach them and start a conversation. This simple act of empathy can make a world of difference to someone who might be feeling out of place or anxious.

In professional settings, social awareness has helped me navigate difficult conversations with empathy and grace. If I need to give critical feedback, for example, I approach the conversation with an understanding of the person's emotional state and choose my words carefully, aiming to be constructive rather than critical.

Understanding social cues and group dynamics has made me more adaptable in different social environments, whether I'm leading a meeting, attending a social event, or simply engaging in casual conversations. It has enhanced my ability to connect with others and create an environment where people feel seen, heard, and understood.

Conclusion: Social Awareness as a Tool for Connection

Developing social awareness has been one of the most transformative aspects of my emotional intelligence journey. It's allowed me to become more attuned to the needs, emotions, and unspoken dynamics of those around me. By learning to read non-verbal cues, understand group dynamics, build rapport, and navigate social situations with empathy, I've strengthened my relationships and created more meaningful connections.

Social awareness isn't just about being aware of others—it's about using that awareness to create positive interactions and foster an environment where everyone feels valued. As you continue to develop your emotional intelligence, I encourage you to practice these skills and see how they transform your relationships, both personally and professionally.

Chapter 7: Emotional Intelligence in Leadership

Leadership is about more than directing tasks and achieving goals—it's about understanding people. Emotional intelligence (EQ) is a fundamental tool for anyone in a leadership role. In this chapter, we will explore how EQ makes leaders more effective in inspiring, motivating, and guiding their teams toward success.

Leading with Empathy

One of the hallmarks of great leadership is empathy—the ability to put yourself in someone else's shoes and see the world from their perspective. Empathetic leaders are attuned to the emotions, concerns, and challenges of their team members, and they respond in ways that show they care.

I've seen firsthand how leading with empathy creates a culture of trust and loyalty. When I once worked with a team facing high levels of burnout, instead of pushing them harder to meet deadlines, I took the time to sit down with each member, listening carefully to their challenges and frustrations. As I empathized with their struggles, we collaboratively sought solutions that balanced the team's well-being with the project demands. The result? Morale improved, productivity soared, and the team felt valued.

Empathy is a powerful motivator. When people feel heard and understood, they are more likely to give their best, stay engaged, and remain committed to the organization. Empathetic leaders foster loyalty and drive a deeper connection within the team, encouraging a strong sense of belonging.

How to Lead with Empathy:

1. **Active Listening**: Make it a habit to actively listen to your team members. This means fully engaging in the conversation, maintaining eye contact, and offering thoughtful responses.

2. **Show Genuine Concern**: People can tell when concern is superficial. Be sincere in your interest in their well-being and make efforts to offer support where possible.

3. **Adapt Your Leadership Style**: Recognize that every person is different. Some need more guidance, while others prefer autonomy. Empathy allows you to understand these preferences and adapt your leadership style accordingly.

By leading with empathy, you not only elevate the performance of your team but also create an environment of trust and mutual respect, where individuals feel valued and understood. This foundation is critical for long-term success in any leadership position.

Decision-Making with Emotional Intelligence

Effective decision-making is at the heart of leadership, and emotional intelligence plays a critical role in making sound, balanced choices. Leaders often face high-stakes decisions that affect their teams, businesses, and personal lives. In such moments, being emotionally aware and in control is key to avoiding impulsive reactions and choosing the best course of action.

In my own leadership journey, I've found that emotional regulation—pausing to assess my feelings—helps me make more rational, thoughtful decisions. Early in my career, I once rushed into a business deal because of the pressure I felt to succeed quickly. The emotional tension clouded my judgment, and I failed to see the warning signs of a risky investment. That experience taught me the importance of stepping back, calming my emotions, and reviewing the facts with a clearer mind before making decisions. Emotional intelligence helped me develop this crucial skill of self-regulation.

How EQ Enhances Decision-Making:

1. **Self-Awareness**: Understanding your emotional state helps you recognize when you're too emotionally charged to make a rational decision. Self-aware leaders are more likely to pause and assess their emotions before proceeding.

2. **Emotional Regulation**: Emotionally intelligent leaders can manage their impulses and not let stress, fear, or excitement drive them to make premature decisions. Taking the time to regulate emotions ensures better long-term outcomes.

3. **Empathy in Decision-Making**: Being aware of how your choices affect others is essential for leadership. Empathetic leaders consider how their decisions will impact team morale, relationships, and overall harmony within the group.

4. **Balanced Perspective**: EQ helps leaders view situations from multiple perspectives, incorporating both emotional insight and logical reasoning. This combination leads to decisions that are not only effective but also compassionate.

By integrating emotional intelligence into decision-making processes, leaders can ensure that their decisions are thoughtful, fair, and beneficial for the long-term success of their teams and organizations.

Building Emotionally Intelligent Teams

An emotionally intelligent leader is only as effective as the team they nurture and guide. A strong, emotionally intelligent team doesn't just function better—it thrives. In today's workplace, where collaboration and connection are key to success, fostering emotional intelligence within teams is essential for high performance, trust, and resilience.

When I first began leading teams, I made the mistake of focusing solely on technical skills and results. It took time to realize that the true engine behind a successful team is the emotional atmosphere—how people feel about their work and each other. Once I started prioritizing emotional intelligence within my team, I saw a dramatic improvement not just in our results, but in the satisfaction and engagement of my team members.

Key Strategies for Building Emotionally Intelligent Teams:

1. **Model Emotional Intelligence**: As a leader, you set the emotional tone for your team. By demonstrating empathy, self-awareness, and emotional regulation, you encourage others to do the same. When team members see you handle stress calmly, communicate openly, and listen with empathy, they are more likely to mirror those behaviors.

2. **Encourage Open Communication**: Emotionally intelligent teams thrive on honest and open communication. Encourage your team members to express their thoughts and feelings without fear of judgment. Create a culture where feedback is welcomed and where everyone's voice is heard. This leads to more transparency, better conflict resolution, and stronger relationships within the team.

3. **Foster Trust and Connection**: Trust is the foundation of a high-performing team, and trust is built through emotional connection. Encourage team-building activities

that help members understand each other on a deeper level. When people feel valued and emotionally connected, they are more motivated to collaborate and support each other.

4. **Promote Empathy and Compassion**: A team that shows empathy towards one another is stronger in the face of challenges. Encourage your team to put themselves in each other's shoes, to understand diverse perspectives, and to offer support when needed. Empathy breaks down barriers and fosters a more inclusive, harmonious work environment.

5. **Provide Emotional Support**: Recognize that your team members will face personal and professional struggles. Acknowledging these challenges and offering support—whether it's flexibility during tough times or simply listening—shows that you care about their well-being, not just their productivity.

Building emotionally intelligent teams leads to better collaboration, increased morale, and greater long-term success. When team members feel emotionally supported, they are more likely to take risks, innovate, and push through obstacles together.

Chapter 8: Lifelong EQ Growth

Continuous Self-Reflection

Emotional intelligence is not a skill you simply acquire and then set aside. It's a lifelong practice that requires ongoing self-reflection and improvement. Throughout my journey of developing emotional intelligence, I've found that the more I learn, the more I realize how much room there is for growth. Emotional intelligence, like any other aspect of personal development, is not a destination but a journey that continues for life.

One of the most powerful tools in this journey is **self-reflection**. Regularly reflecting on your actions, emotions, and interactions helps you gain deeper insights into how you function emotionally and how you relate to others. It allows you to identify patterns of behavior that may be holding you back and gives you the clarity to make positive changes.

In the early stages of my personal EQ journey, I would take time at the end of each day to reflect on moments when my emotions were heightened—both positive and negative. I would ask myself questions like: What triggered my reaction? Could I have responded differently? How did my response impact the people around me? This daily practice gave me the insight I needed to understand my emotional triggers and tendencies. Over time, it helped me become more self-aware and better equipped to manage my emotions in real-time.

Here are a few techniques that can help you maintain continuous self-reflection:

1. **Daily Journaling**: Writing down your thoughts and emotions at the end of each day can help you process experiences and gain clarity about your emotional patterns. Focus on how you felt in certain situations, why you responded in a certain way, and what you could learn from the experience.

2. **Regular Check-ins**: Set aside time to check in with yourself periodically. This can be as simple as taking a few moments during the day to ask yourself, "How am I feeling right now?" or "What's causing stress or joy in this moment?" These check-ins build self-awareness and help you stay grounded in your emotions.

3. **Seek Feedback**: Sometimes, the best way to understand yourself is through the eyes of others. Ask trusted friends, family, or colleagues for feedback on how you handle emotions, manage relationships, or respond to stress. Honest, constructive feedback can give you a clearer view of your strengths and areas for improvement.

4. **Meditation and Mindfulness**: These practices promote self-awareness by encouraging you to observe your thoughts and emotions without judgment. Mindfulness helps you stay present, which is essential for recognizing and managing emotions in the moment.

The key to continuous growth in emotional intelligence is to embrace the process. Self-reflection is not about being hard on yourself or dwelling on mistakes. Instead, it's about learning from your experiences and using those lessons to move forward. When you commit to regular self-reflection, you'll find that your emotional awareness and control will continue to improve, leading to deeper, more fulfilling relationships and a greater sense of emotional well-being.

Practicing Emotional Intelligence Daily

Developing emotional intelligence is not just about reflecting on our emotions or managing our reactions in moments of crisis. It's about weaving emotionally intelligent practices into the fabric of our daily lives. When we integrate EQ into everyday routines, it becomes a natural part of how we navigate the world and connect with others.

Personally, I found that the small, intentional choices I made throughout the day had a profound impact on my emotional intelligence growth. Over time, I learned that these simple practices, when done consistently, helped me stay more in tune with myself and others, reinforcing my self-awareness, empathy, and emotional control.

Here are some practical ways to make EQ a part of your daily life:

1. Start Each Day with Emotional Check-Ins

Taking just a few moments at the start of the day to check in with yourself can set a positive tone for the rest of your day. Ask yourself, "How am I feeling right now? What emotions am I carrying into the day?" Recognizing your emotional state early on helps you stay self-aware, which is the foundation of emotional intelligence. It also prepares you to handle challenges more thoughtfully.

2. Pause Before Reacting

I've come to value the power of a pause before reacting to emotionally charged situations. Whether it's a difficult conversation with a colleague or a sudden frustration at home, giving yourself a moment to breathe allows you to respond rather than react. This pause can be as simple as taking a few deep breaths, giving your brain time to process your emotions, and choosing how you want to act.

3. Practice Active Listening

Listening is one of the most important ways to show empathy. In my experience, people often just want to feel heard and understood. When I started focusing more on listening to understand, rather than simply waiting for my turn to speak, I found my relationships deepened. Try focusing on what others are saying without distractions, asking questions to clarify, and responding in a way that shows genuine interest and care.

4. Use Gratitude as a Tool

Practicing gratitude is not just a feel-good exercise—it's a powerful way to stay connected to positive emotions. I've made it a habit to reflect on the things I'm grateful for at the end of each day. Sometimes it's something small, like enjoying a good meal, and other times it's the people in my life. This habit keeps me grounded and helps me focus on the positive aspects of life, boosting both my emotional intelligence and resilience.

5. Manage Stress Proactively

Stress is inevitable, but how we manage it is key to maintaining emotional balance. I've found that recognizing the early signs of stress—like feeling irritable or overwhelmed—allows me to take action before it escalates. Simple practices like deep breathing, short walks, or even a few minutes of meditation can make a world of difference in bringing stress levels down.

6. Acknowledge Your Progress

Growth in emotional intelligence, like any personal development, happens in small, consistent steps. Every time you pause to reflect on your emotions, show empathy to someone, or manage a stressful moment calmly, you're reinforcing your emotional intelligence. Celebrate these small wins. They may seem minor, but over time, they add up to significant growth.

By practicing these simple habits regularly, you'll notice that emotional intelligence becomes more natural to you.

It's not something that only comes into play during difficult moments—it becomes part of your daily approach to life. As you continue to strengthen these habits, your emotional intelligence will grow, and you'll find that both your personal and professional relationships benefit from it.

Final Words of Encouragement

As we come to the end of this journey together, I want to remind you that developing emotional intelligence is not an overnight transformation. It is a lifelong practice, one that requires patience, persistence, and a genuine commitment to self-growth. There will be moments where progress feels slow or even stagnant, but remember, every small step you take contributes to your overall development.

Personally, I've experienced how challenging it can be to maintain emotional balance in the face of adversity. There were times when I faltered, reacting impulsively or struggling to understand the emotions of those around me. But with time, and through consistent practice, I noticed how my ability to navigate difficult situations improved. I became more aware of my triggers, better at managing my emotions, and more empathetic in my relationships.

I want to encourage you to stay the course. Whether you are striving to become a more emotionally intelligent leader, strengthen your personal relationships, or simply grow in self-awareness, know that every effort you put into this journey matters. The beauty of emotional intelligence is that it enhances not just your life but the lives of those you interact with. It builds bridges of understanding, compassion, and trust, which are the foundation of meaningful relationships.

As you move forward, keep in mind these three key takeaways:

1. **Self-awareness is the foundation**: Always start by understanding yourself—your emotions, your triggers, and your patterns. The more in tune you are with your internal world, the more effectively you can navigate the external world.

2. **Empathy strengthens connections**: In both personal and professional settings, empathy is the key to building deeper, more meaningful relationships. It allows you to understand others on a deeper level and respond to them in a way that fosters trust and respect.

3. **Emotional intelligence is a journey**: There is no final destination. As you grow and evolve, so will your emotional intelligence. Embrace the process, be kind to yourself when you stumble, and celebrate the small victories along the way.

In closing, remember that emotional intelligence is one of the most valuable skills you can cultivate. It has the power to transform your life and the lives of those around you. So, take the first step, and continue to practice every day. With time, dedication, and perseverance, you will unlock the full potential of your emotional intelligence and create a more fulfilling, connected, and emotionally rich life.

Call to Action

Thank you for taking the time to embark on this journey toward mastering emotional intelligence. I truly hope that the insights and techniques shared in this book have inspired you to take active steps in cultivating your own emotional intelligence and applying it to every aspect of your life.

Now that you've gained a deeper understanding of EQ and its profound impact on personal and professional success, I encourage you to put these lessons into practice. Start with small steps—whether it's pausing before reacting, practicing empathy in your conversations, or dedicating time to self-reflection each day. These small actions will accumulate into significant changes over time.

Here's how you can continue this journey:

- **Reflect and Share**: Take time to reflect on how emotional intelligence has impacted your relationships, career, and personal growth. If you found this book helpful, consider sharing your thoughts and experiences with others. Leave a review online or recommend the book to someone who may benefit from developing their own EQ.

- **Stay Connected**: Emotional intelligence is an ongoing process of learning and growth. Follow me on social media for regular tips, discussions, and updates on how to further develop emotional intelligence. Let's continue this conversation and support each other in becoming more emotionally intelligent individuals.

- **Apply What You've Learned**: The true power of emotional intelligence lies in its application. Whether it's leading with empathy in the workplace, managing conflict with grace in personal relationships, or simply becoming more attuned to your own emotional world, take what you've learned and implement it into your daily life. Remember, real change comes from action.

- **Join a Community**: Consider joining or starting an emotional intelligence group or accountability circle where you can regularly discuss EQ topics, share your experiences, and support each other in your growth journeys.

You've already made the first, most important step by prioritizing your emotional intelligence. Keep going. With persistence, reflection, and commitment, you will continue to see your life, relationships, and career transform in powerful ways.

Thank you once again for allowing me to be a part of your journey. Stay curious, stay compassionate, and above all, keep growing.

Author's Note

When I first began exploring the concept of emotional intelligence, I was struck by how profoundly it can impact every facet of our lives. The ability to understand, regulate, and harness emotions, both our own and others', is not just a skill—it's a superpower. Emotional intelligence shapes the way we connect with people, how we lead, and how we handle life's inevitable ups and downs.

Writing this book has been a deeply personal and enlightening journey for me. I've drawn from my own experiences, as well as the experiences of others, to bring you a comprehensive guide to developing emotional intelligence. My goal was to create a resource that not only explains the importance of EQ but also provides actionable steps for enhancing it in your day-to-day life.

Emotional intelligence isn't a static trait, nor is it something you either have or you don't. It's a skill set that can be cultivated, refined, and grown over time. Whether you're navigating the complexities of relationships, striving for success in your career, or simply trying to understand yourself better, emotional intelligence is a tool that will serve you well in every context.

I hope that the ideas, strategies, and insights shared in this book inspire you to reflect on your own emotional landscape and take steps toward greater emotional awareness, control, and empathy. Remember, the journey toward emotional intelligence is ongoing. It requires effort, patience, and practice. But the rewards—stronger relationships, more effective leadership, and a deeper sense of fulfillment—are well worth it.

Thank you for choosing to embark on this journey with me. I hope this book serves as a valuable companion in your pursuit of emotional growth, and that it helps you unlock the full potential of your emotional intelligence.

Wishing you success and growth,

Anil Solanki

Contact Information

Thank you for your interest in **"The Emotion Code:Unlocking the Power of Emotional Intelligence"** I welcome your feedback, questions, and insights regarding the book or any of the topics discussed within. Please feel free to reach out to me through the following channels:

- Email:

ani.royalmanagement@gmail.com

- Website:

www.anilsolankijaat.com

- Social Media:

  - **Instagram**: [@jaatanilsolanki](https://www.instagram.com/jaatanilsolanki)
  - **Facebook**: [facebook.com/jaatanilsolanki](https://www.facebook.com/jaatanilsolanki)

I look forward to connecting with you and hearing your thoughts on the book. Your journey toward transforming habits and achieving personal growth inspires me, and I'm here to support you along the way!

Made in the USA
Las Vegas, NV
12 March 2025

19468423R00049